WOODWIND QUARTET
SCORE AND PARTS
-FLUTE
-OBOE
-CLARINET
-BASSOON

I0620528

10 CHRISTMAS SONGS FOR WOODWIND QUARTET

JEFF BRATZ

HARMONYTABS

Sign up for the HarmonyTabs email list to keep up with new music releases, upcoming publications, and promotions:

HARMONYTABS EMAIL LIST

10 CHRISTMAS SONGS FOR WOODWIND QUARTET
SECOND EDITION
Copyright © 2025 Jeff Bratz

To request permission, contact the publisher at publishing@HarmonyTabsMusic.com

ISBN: 978-1-961735-26-2 (paperback)
ISBN: 978-1-961735-27-9 (eBook)
ISMN: 979-0-60026-099-7 (paperback)
ISMN: 979-0-60026-100-0 (eBook)

First paperback edition October 2022

Printed in the United States of America

HarmonyTabs Music

HarmonyTabsMusic.com

CONTENTS

INTRO

First, thank you for buying this songbook. I know there are a lot of options out there and I'm honored you landed here.

I hope these songs will be as fun for you to play through as they were for me to arrange. I've always loved the holiday season and I think that's largely due to the music that fills the air in every store, car, home, and everywhere else. I like to believe that in some small part this book will add to the spirit.

On the last page of the score and on each part is a QR code. That code will lead you to a homepage for that song where you can find additional resources including audio/video where you can hear the tune and find optional rehearsal tracks.

If at any point you have any questions, comments, suggestions, or anything else, please feel free to drop me a line: Jeff@HarmonyTabs.com.

Happy music-ing!
-Jeff

ANGELS WE HAVE HEARD ON HIGH

Traditional French Carol
Arr. Jeff Bratz

AWHHOH (WQ)
11-11-2024

ANGELS WE HAVE HEARD ON HIGH

ANGELS WE HAVE HEARD ON HIGH

AWHHOH (WQ)
11-11-2024

ANGELS WE HAVE HEARD ON HIGH

Flute

Traditional French Carol
Arr. Jeff Bratz

AWHHOH (WQ)
11-11-2024

- 4 -

Additional resources for this arrangement

ANGELS WE HAVE HEARD ON HIGH

Oboe

Traditional French Carol
Arr. Jeff Bratz

Additional resources for this arrangement

- 5 -

AWHHOH (WQ)
11-11-2024

ANGELS WE HAVE HEARD ON HIGH

Clarinet

Traditional French Carol
Arr. Jeff Bratz

AWHHOH (WQ)
11-11-2024

Additional
resources for
this arrangement

ANGELS WE HAVE HEARD ON HIGH

Bassoon

Traditional French Carol
Arr. Jeff Bratz

©2019 HarmonyTabs Music
www.HarmonyTabsMusic.com
ISMN: 979-0-60026-101-7

- 7 -

AWHHOH (WQ)
11-11-2024

Additional resources for this arrangement

AULD LANG SYNE

Poem by Robert Burns
Arr. Jeff Bratz

ALS (WQ)
11-11-24

©2018 HarmonyTabs Music
www.HarmonyTabsMusic.com
ISMN: 979-0-60026-102-4

AULD LANG SYNE

ALS (WQ)
11-11-24

AULD LANG SYNE

Flute

Poem by Robert Burns
Arr. Jeff Bratz

- 10 -

Additional resources for this arrangement

Oboe

AULD LANG SYNE

Poem by Robert Burns
Arr. Jeff Bratz

ALS (WQ)
11-11-24

AULD LANG SYNE

Clarinet

Poem by Robert Burns
Arr. Jeff Bratz

ALS (WQ)
11-11-24

Additional resources for this arrangement

AULD LANG SYNE

Bassoon

Poem by Robert Burns
Arr. Jeff Bratz

Additional resources for this arrangement

ALS (WQ)
11-11-24

AWAY IN A MANGER

William J. Kirkpatrick
and James R. Murray
Arr. Jeff Bratz

AIAM (WQ)
11-15-24

- 14 -

AWAY IN A MANGER

AIAM (WQ)
11-15-24

AWAY IN A MANGER

AWAY IN A MANGER

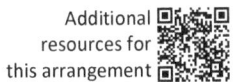

AIAM (WQ)
11-15-24

AWAY IN A MANGER

Flute

William J. Kirkpatrick
and James R. Murray
Arr. Jeff Bratz

- 18 -

AWAY IN A MANGER

William J. Kirkpatrick
and James R. Murray
Arr. Jeff Bratz

Oboe

AIAM (WQ)
11-15-24

- 19 -

AWAY IN A MANGER

Clarinet

William J. Kirkpatrick
and James R. Murray
Arr. Jeff Bratz

AIAM (WQ)
11-15-24

All Rights Reserved
©2019 HarmonyTabs Music
www.HarmonyTabsMusic.com
ISMN: 979-0-60026-103-1

AWAY IN A MANGER

Bassoon

William J. Kirkpatrick
and James R. Murray
Arr. Jeff Bratz

Additional resources for this arrangement

AIAM (WQ)
11-15-24

DECK THE HALLS

Traditional Welsh Carol
Arr. Jeff Bratz

DTH (WQ)
11-15-24

DECK THE HALLS

DTH (WQ)
11-15-24

DECK THE HALLS

DTH (WQ)
11-15-24

DECK THE HALLS

DECK THE HALLS

Flute

Traditional Welsh Carol
Arr. Jeff Bratz

DTH (WQ)
11-15-24

DECK THE HALLS

DECK THE HALLS

Oboe

Traditional Welsh Carol
Arr. Jeff Bratz

DTH (WQ)
11-15-24

DECK THE HALLS

DECK THE HALLS

Clarinet

Traditional Welsh Carol
Arr. Jeff Bratz
SWING

DTH (WQ)
11-15-24

Clarinet
DECK THE HALLS

DTH (WQ)
11-15-24

Additional
resources for
this arrangement

DECK THE HALLS

Bassoon

Traditional Welsh Carol
Arr. Jeff Bratz

DTH (WQ)
11-15-24

Bassoon
DECK THE HALLS

DTH (WQ)
11-15-24

THE FIRST NOEL

Traditional English Carol
Arr. Jeff Bratz

TFN (WQ)
11-21-24

THE FIRST NOEL

THE FIRST NOEL

TFN (WQ)
11-21-24

THE FIRST NOEL

TFN (WQ)
11-21-24

Additional resources for this arrangement

THE FIRST NOEL

Traditional English Carol
Arr. Jeff Bratz

Flute

All Rights Reserved
©2019 HarmonyTabs Music
www.HarmonyTabsMusic.com
ISMN: 979-0-60026-110-9

- 39 -

TFN (WQ)
11-21-24

THE FIRST NOEL

Oboe

Traditional English Carol
Arr. Jeff Bratz

TFN (WQ)
11-21-24

Additional
resources for
this arrangement

THE FIRST NOEL

Clarinet

Traditional English Carol
Arr. Jeff Bratz

TFN (WQ)
11-21-24

Bassoon

THE FIRST NOEL

Traditional English Carol
Arr. Jeff Bratz

TFN (WQ)
11-21-24

Additional
resources for
this arrangement

GO TELL IT ON THE MOUNTAIN

COMPILED BY
JOHN WESLEY WORK, JR.
ARR. JEFF BRATZ

- 43 -

GTIOTM (WQ)
11-21-24

GO TELL IT ON THE MOUNTAIN

GT1OTM (WQ)
11-21-24

GO TELL IT ON THE MOUNTAIN

GT10Tm (WQ)
11-21-24

Flute

GO TELL IT ON THE MOUNTAIN

COMPILED BY
JOHN WESLEY WORK, JR.
ARR. JEFF BRATZ

♩=100 SWING

mf

5

9   TO CODA

13

17   D.S. AL CODA

21 CODA   N.B.

23

27

31

- 47 -

GT1OTM (WQ)
11-21-24

GO TELL IT ON THE MOUNTAIN

Oboe

COMPILED BY
JOHN WESLEY WORK, JR.
ARR. JEFF BRATZ

GT1OTM (WQ)
11-21-24

- 48 -

Additional resources for this arrangement

GO TELL IT ON THE MOUNTAIN

Clarinet

COMPILED BY
JOHN WESLEY WORK, JR.
ARR. JEFF BRATZ

ALL RIGHTS RESERVED
©2019 HarmonyTabs Music
www.HarmonyTabsMusic.com
ISMN: 979-0-60026-105-5

GT10TM (WQ)
11-21-24

- 49 -

GO TELL IT ON THE MOUNTAIN

Bassoon

Compiled by
John Wesley Work, Jr.
Arr. Jeff Bratz

GTIOTM (WQ)
11-21-24

All Rights Reserved
©2019 HarmonyTabs Music
www.HarmonyTabsMusic.com
ISMN: 979-0-60026-105-5

GOD REST YE MERRY, GENTLEMEN

19th Century English Carol
Arr. Jeff Bratz

GRYMG (WQ)
11-22-24

GOD REST YE MERRY, GENTLEMEN

GRYMG (WQ)
11-22-24

GOD REST YE MERRY, GENTLEMEN

GRYMG (WQ)
11-22-24

GOD REST YE MERRY, GENTLEMEN

Flute

19th Century English Carol
Arr. Jeff Bratz

- 55 -

GRYMG (WQ)
11-22-24

GOD REST YE MERRY, GENTLEMEN

GRYMG (WQ)
11-22-24

GOD REST YE MERRY, GENTLEMEN

Oboe

19th Century English Carol
Arr. Jeff Bratz

GRYMG (WQ)
11-22-24

GOD REST YE MERRY, GENTLEMEN

GOD REST YE MERRY, GENTLEMEN

Clarinet

19th Century English Carol
Arr. Jeff Bratz

GRYMG (WQ)
11-22-24

GOD REST YE MERRY, GENTLEMEN

GRYMG (WQ)
11-22-24

GOD REST YE MERRY, GENTLEMEN

Bassoon

19th Century English Carol
Arr. Jeff Bratz

GRYMG (WQ)
11-22-24

GOD REST YE MERRY, GENTLEMEN

GRYmG (WQ)
11-22-24

HALLELUJAH CHORUS
(ABRIDGED)

George Friedrich Handel
Arr. Jeff Bratz

©2018 HarmonyTabs Music
www.HarmonyTabsMusic.com
ISMN: 979-0-60026-107-9

HC (WQ)
12-5-24

HALLELUJAH CHORUS (ABRIDGED)

HALLELUJAH CHORUS (ABRIDGED)

HALLELUJAH CHORUS (ABRIDGED)

HC (WQ)
12-5-24

HALLELUJAH CHORUS
(ABRIDGED)

Flute

George Friedrich Handel
Arr. Jeff Bratz

Additional resources for this arrangement

HC (WQ)
12-5-24

HALLELUJAH CHORUS
(ABRIDGED)

Oboe

George Friedrich Handel
arr. Jeff Bratz

©2018 HarmonyTabs Music
www.HarmonyTabsMusic.com
ISMN: 979-0-60026-107-9

HC (WQ)
12-5-24

- 68 -

Additional resources for this arrangement

HALLELUJAH CHORUS
(ABRIDGED)

Clarinet

George Friedrich Handel
arr. Jeff Bratz

Additional resources for this arrangement

HC (WQ)
12-5-24

Bassoon

HALLELUJAH CHORUS
(ABRIDGED)

George Friedrich Handel
arr. Jeff Bratz

HC (WQ)
12-5-24

Additional
resources for
this arrangement

HARK! THE HERALD ANGELS SING

Felix Mendelssohn
Lyrics by Charles Wesley
and George Whitefield
Arr. Jeff Bratz

HTHAS (WQ)
12-16-24

HARK! THE HERALD ANGELS SING

HTHAS (WQ)
12-16-24

HARK! THE HERALD ANGELS SING

HTHAS (WQ)
12-16-24

HARK! THE HERALD ANGELS SING

Flute

Felix Mendelssohn
Lyrics by Charles Wesley
and George Whitefield
Arr. Jeff Bratz

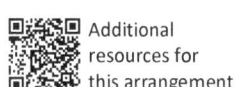

HTHAS (WQ)
12-16-24

HARK! THE HERALD ANGELS SING

Oboe

Felix Mendelssohn
Lyrics by Charles Wesley
and George Whitefield
Arr. Jeff Bratz

HTHAS (WQ)
12-16-24

Additional resources for this arrangement

HARK! THE HERALD ANGELS SING

Clarinet

Felix Mendelssohn
Lyrics by Charles Wesley
and George Whitefield
Arr. Jeff Bratz

Additional
resources for
this arrangement

- 77 -

HTHAS (WQ)
12-16-24

HARK! THE HERALD ANGELS SING

Bassoon

Felix Mendelssohn
Lyrics by Charles Wesley
and George Whitefield
Arr. Jeff Bratz

HTHAS (WQ)
12-16-24

Additional
resources for
this arrangement

I SAW THREE SHIPS

Traditional
Arr. Jeff Bratz

ISTS (WQ)
12-17-24

I SAW THREE SHIPS

I SAW THREE SHIPS

ISTS (WQ)
12-17-24

I SAW THREE SHIPS

I SAW THREE SHIPS

ISTS (WQ)
12-17-24

I SAW THREE SHIPS

Flute

Traditional
Arr. Jeff Bratz

ISTS (WQ)
12-17-24

FLUTE
I SAW THREE SHIPS

ISTS (WQ)
12-17-24

I SAW THREE SHIPS

Oboe

Traditional
Arr. Jeff Bratz

ISTS (WQ)
12-17-24

Oboe
I SAW THREE SHIPS

ISTS (WQ)
12-17-24

I SAW THREE SHIPS

Clarinet

Traditional
Arr. Jeff Bratz

ISTS (WQ)
12-17-24

CLARINET
I SAW THREE SHIPS

ISTS (WQ)
12-17-24

I SAW THREE SHIPS

Bassoon

Traditional
Arr. Jeff Bratz

ISTS (WQ)
12-17-24

I SAW THREE SHIPS

ISTS (WQ)
12-17-24

FINAL WORDS

Please consider leaving a review of this book. I would greatly appreciate it. It will help me to continue on this book writing journey I've set off on.

Thank you in advance!

LEAVE A REVIEW

HARMONYTABS EMAIL LIST

Once again, here is the link to the HarmonyTabs email list to keep you up to speed on any new music, publications, and promotions.

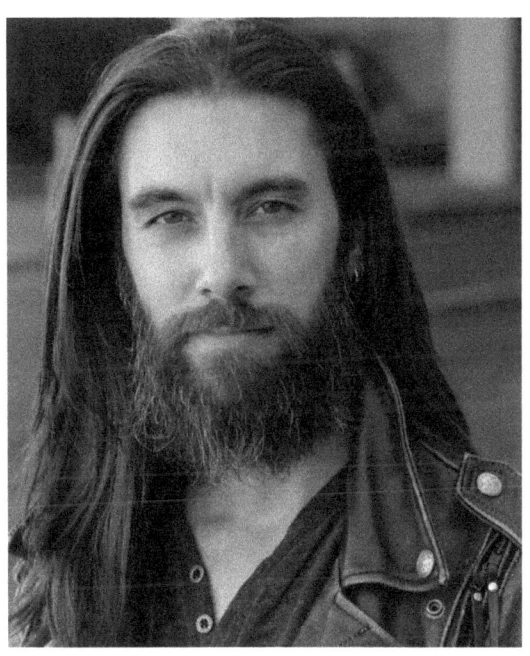

ABOUT THE AUTHOR

Jeff Bratz has a degree in Professional Music from the School for Music Vocations and a Professional Certificate in Music Theory and Composition from Berklee College of Music. He's a composer and arranger specializing in vocal arrangements. In a former life, Jeff was a music teacher for grades pre-k through high school. He has sung in dozens of vocal groups including The Dickens Carolers at Disneyland's *Club 33*, The Fault Line on *America's Got Talent*, and Manhattan Transfer tribute group LA Transfer. He was also part of the Downbeat award-winning First Take. He currently performs with rock band RaDIUM, 80s rock tribute band 8IGHTY 6IXX, and salsa band Calle Mambo. He lives in Massachusetts with his wonderful partner Kristen and the cutest nugget that ever nuggeted: Ollie!

Also Available From

HarmonyTabs

Sheet Music

-A Cappella Choirs/Groups
-Brass Ensembles
-String Ensembles
-Sax Ensembles
And More!

HARMONYTABS.COM/SHEET-MUSIC/

Songbooks

-Wind Ensembles
-A Cappella Choirs/Groups
-Flute Ensembles
-Brass Ensembles
And More!

HARMONYTABS.COM/MUSIC-BOOKS/SONGBOOKS/

Music Theory and Instruction

-An Incomplete Crash Course
in Contemporary Music Theory:
The Fundamentals

More to Come!

HARMONYTABS.COM/MUSIC-BOOKS/INSTRUCTIONAL-BOOKS/

Music Composition

-Standard Manuscript Notebook
-Pocket Manuscript Notebook
-Writing Prompt Journals

More to Come!

HARMONYTABS.COM/MUSIC-BOOKS/MUSIC-COMPOSITION-BOOKS/

HarmonyTabsMusic.com